SEMINAR

BY THERESA REBECK

Productions in Print

An In An Hour Book
www.inanhourbooks.com
An imprint of Smith and Kraus Publishers, Inc.
Published by Smith and Kraus, Inc.
177 Lyme Road, Hanover, NH 03755
www.SmithandKraus.com

Manufactured in the United States of America

Cover Design: Serino/Coyne
Interior Layout: Nathan Spring

ISBN-13: 978-1-57525-810-2   ISBN-10: 1-57525-810-2

10 9 8 7 6 5 4 3 2 1

• Essay from the Playwright •

I've had my own experiences with really brutal teachers. Remembering all the times I had my heart stomped on by a powerful figure whose approval I desperately wanted, it just seemed like an innately terrifying and hilarious situation. And I guess, from that, came *Seminar*. Though if I'm being fully honest, I also just thought it could be funny to see a really, really gifted actor in his fifties take apart a bunch of actors in their twenties.

We were blessed with a first rate cast for *Seminar*'s first production. Each actor brought a lot to the table and because of that the play gained an enormous wealth of humanity in rehearsal, and we were not sure it was funny anymore. And we were okay with that, because in a lot of ways, it's a very fascinating and humane play about these people and their desperation and their passion. When an audience saw it for the first time and roared with laughter, it was a shock and a wonderful reminder that, "Yeah, these terrifying situations are full of comedy."

I think the play hold it's own up there—audiences are responding to its humor and its heart. The play is about the dream of being an artist and how confusing it is to achieve a sense of that in a world that defines art so narrowly, in capitalistic terms, which belittles the spiritual realities of art.

Theresa Rebeck

Jerry O' Connell, Hettienne Park and **Lily Rabe** in a scene from "Seminar" on Broadway at the Golden Theatre. Photo: Jeremy Daniel.

Hamish Linklater and **Alan Rickman,** in a scene from "Seminar" on Broadway at the Golden Theatre. Photo: Jeremy Daniel.

• Essay from the Broadway Producer •

Conventional wisdom says you should never open a new play cold on Broadway; especially a comedy that has never had the benefit of an audience reaction or been reviewed by a critic. To go through the rehearsal process without hearing audience laughter is (at moments) an excruciating and unnerving experience. Nevertheless, when you trust the material and collaborate with a talented and dynamic team, a confidence guides you to conquer fear and produce something fresh. I feel fortunate to have had that experience with *Seminar*.

For me, a great play starts with the characters and their story. Theresa's witty and insightful script instantly caught my attention. *Seminar* is a play about writers struggling to fulfill their creative vision. It is also a play about the strength of the human spirit, what we sacrifice to achieve our goals, and the compromises life forces us to face on the road to success. *Seminar* is immensely smart, contemporary, engaging and heartbreaking, inspiring, and - from the first scene - laugh out loud funny. I knew this play deserved a world premiere on Broadway; and I hope you enjoy reading it as much as I did the very first time.

Jeffrey Finn

SEMINAR

• THE OPENING NIGHT CAST WAS •
(in order of speaking)

Douglas . . . . Jerry O'Connell
Martin . . . . Hamish Linklater
Kate . . . . Lily Rabe
Izzy . . . . Hettienne Park
Leonard . . . . Alan Rickman

Seminar is performed without an intermission

Seminar opened on Broadway on November 20, 2011 and was presented by Jeffrey Finn, Jill Furman, John N. Hart Jr. and Patrick Milling Smith, Roy Furman, David Ian, David Mirvish, Amy Nauiokas, and James Spry, with associate producers Matthew Schneider, Wake Up Marconi, Jamie Kaye-Phillips, and Charles Stone/Ben Limberg. The executive producer/general manager was 101 Productions, LTD. The production played the John Golden Theatre.

Sam Gold directed the play. Scenic and costume design was by David Zinn, lighting design was by Ben Stanton, original music and sound design was by John Gromada; the casting was by MelCap Casting, the production manager was Peter Fulbright, the production stage manager was Charles Means.

Alan Rickman in a scene from "Seminar" on Broadway at the Golden theatre. Photo: Jeremy Daniel

Scene One

An apartment. Izzy, Martin, Kate and Douglas.

DOUGLAS
I mean the place is amazing, the grounds are completely, like it's this astonishingly sculpted landscape, where everything seems to be sculpted out of trees and water so that interiority and exteriority meet, you know, what you are surrounded by is this exquisite, idealized just completely perfect environment---

Martin, behind him, can't stand all this.

DOUGLAS
--and the buildings almost hover over the grass, like on a hot summer day when the air is so warm that it's tangible, the manor seems to hover and there's so much, the trees are so present that you can feel them growing, I'm not kidding! You start to realize that medieval conceptions of magic frankly must have just been completely based in a kind of reality, that things were so green and growing that all the time, it must have seemed a sort of magic, at least that's what it feels like because it was just such a creative environment. Everything so perfectly balanced. The interiority and the exteriority. you know that thing that Indigo Jones was always trying for, there there's such a perfect harmony between the interior and the exterior world that—

MARTIN
(overlapping)
Inigo.
(then)
Inigo.
(then)
INIGO. You said Indigo. It's Inigo.

DOUGLAS
I said Inigo.

MARTIN
No, you said Indigo.

DOUGLAS
I said Inigo.

KATE
It doesn't matter.

MARTIN
Not if you don't care about accuracy in language.

KATE
Come on.

MARTIN
But if you do care about accuracy—

DOUGLAS
I said Inigo.

MARTIN
Then it might matter, a little.

DOUGLAS
Anyway it is an awesome place to write. I mean, MacDowell is good too, it's serious at least, they don't let just anybody in, which is so necessary. I won't go to anyplace except Yaddo or MacDowell anymore. Pretty much everyplace else? Let me tell you, the flavor of the desperation is really not to be believed.

IZZY
What are you working on?

DOUGLAS
A couple of stories, the one that the New Yorker asked to see, I did another draft of that, and my agent had some thoughts about the

novel that I took a look at. He's going out with it next week, so we both thought that I should just take one last pass at it, make sure it was as tight as it could be. I just spewed so much of that thing so there's always hopefully going to be a kind of on the road chaos to the sound. Not on the road, hopefully what I achieved is a little more I don't know, intellectually rigorous than what Kerouac was going for.

MARTIN

Yeah I hope that too. Because 'On the Road' was such a minor achievement.

DOUGLAS

Well, it's not exactly a world masterpiece.

MARTIN

What did you say?

KATE

Could we not talk about Kerouac? He was a complete psychotic pig. Guys love talking about him and girls are bored to death.

DOUGLAS

Well he didn't exactly have a feminist agenda.

IZZY

Thank god for that.

KATE

What? I'm sorry what did you—

IZZY

I just hate all these women who are so hung up about sex.

KATE

So women who don't like Kerouac are 'hung up about sex?'

                              IZZY
You can't deny there's an associative correlation.

                              KATE
I can absolutely deny there's an associative correlation. Kerouac was a misogynistic hack what's that got to do with women who like sex?

                              MARTIN
              (overlap)
No no no no no no

                              IZZY
That's a little reductive.

                              KATE
You said anyone who doesn't like Kerouac is hung up about sex and I'M the one who's reductive?

                              MARTIN
Don't listen to her. She loves him. She reads him in the bathtub. She lights candles and swoons in the bubble bath. "Jack, Jack-- Jaaaaccck--"

        She is laughing. She shoves him. They tussle.

                              IZZY
So you guys like, knew each other before this, right?

                              KATE
High school.

                              MARTIN
              (Chiming in)
High school.

                              IZZY
And you still have a crush on him?

                                KATE
What? No!

                                MARTIN
No!

                                KATE
No!

                                IZZY
Just checking.

                                KATE
So Douglas, your agent thinks that your novel is ready to go out?

                                DOUGLAS
Yeah, he's really optimistic. I mean, you want to be cautious. But
a lot of people saw the story in Tin House so there's just a lot of
interest.

                                IZZY
That story was amazing.

                                DOUGLAS
Thanks.

                                IZZY
Really really elegant.

                                DOUGLAS
Thanks. I was pleased with how it came out. I mean I was so worried
about it, because it was risky, you know, to go that experimental with
the language, people aren't trained anymore to be able to hear it, post
modernism has really fallen on hard times although it's not so much
post modern, really as magical realism. That's more tonally where I
finally ended up, and I think that, at least, people are still open to.
But god! The novel has fallen on hard times, and I'm not talking

about EBooks. EBooks, don't get me started. And on top of it, all anyone wants anymore are memoirs. And I'm not saying, I think it's an interesting form, I'm as curious about the inside of my own brain as anyone but please! Where's the bathroom, Kate, I need to take a piss.

KATE
Oh it's through the door and down the hall.

DOUGLAS
You have doors on the hallways, I love it. No seriously it's fabulous. Your family owns this place?

KATE
We have the lease. As long as one of us, is like you know a direct whatever.

DOUGLAS
Oh god yeah.

MARTIN
As long as one of you is what?

KATE
It's, you know. It's rent controlled, or stabilized, whatever you call it.

MARTIN
No come on, how much.

KATE
It's very affordable.

MARTIN
You're so old New York.

DOUGLAS
Seriously how much?

KATE
I thought you had to pee Douglas.

DOUGLAS
I do. I'm desperate to pee but I'm more desperate to find out how much you pay for this palace.

KATE
It's been in our family a long time.

MARTIN
You don't know?

KATE
Of course I know.

MARTIN
Well then what is it?

KATE
(Beat.)
Eight hundred... dollars.

MARTIN
(Stunned)
Eight hundred dollars?   What do you mean, eight hundred a day?

KATE
Eight hundred a month.

MARTIN
You never told me that.

KATE
It's not that big a deal.

MARTIN

That you have a free apartment on the Upper West Side? How is that not a 'big deal?' I can't believe you never told me this. How have I never heard this?

KATE

It's lucky.

MARTIN

Lucky is a seat on the subway. You have sixteen rooms and a view of the river!

KATE

We have nine rooms! And you can only see the river from two of them.

IZZY

The living room, the dining room and that bedroom—

KATE

Okay three, three rooms have the view.

DOUGLAS

Eight hundred a month. That--is fabulous.

MARTIN

It's socialism for the rich!

KATE

I didn't ask for it!

MARTIN

The rich never do, isn't that funny? People just keep giving them things that they don't ever even ask for!

KATE

Being middle class doesn't make you morally superior, MARTIN!

MARTIN

I'm not middle class. I'm a nobody with a shitty expensive apartment in Queens. And I didn't say it made me 'morally superior.'

KATE

It doesn't make you a better writer, either.

DOUGLAS

No, totally, eight hundred a month, it's like having a grant without having to actually get one. Although grants aren't just about money. You have to be careful, flying too under the radar, people don't like that.

He goes. They all look at each other.

MARTIN

'People don't like that?' What people?

KATE

You have to stop being so mean to him, Martin! He's important!

MARTIN

Holy shit. Indigo Jones. The flavor of the desperation.

KATE

(laughing)
He knows lots of people!

MARTIN

I know lots of people too.

KATE

The people you know are nobodies who majored in English at itty bitty liberal arts colleges on the east coast.

MARTIN

You mean like you?

IZZY

Well, he went to Yaddo! And once you have an in there, you have pull, he could get you into Yaddo!

MARTIN

Where the interiority and the exteriority of the landscape have achieved such a supreme state of harmonic convergence that the whole place is about to lift off.

KATE

You're jealous.

MARTIN

Jealous? Of that?

KATE

You've been rejected by Yaddo three times.

MARTIN

Thank you.

KATE

And McDowell- how many—

MARTIN

Yes thank you. Thank you! I needed to be reminded. Thank you.

IZZY

Well he's been a bunch of times. Plus I'm telling you he's really hooked up. His uncle is like a world famous what was he.

KATE

He was one of the weathermen, one of the terrorists.

IZZY

No. He was a playwright.

KATE

He was a terrorist!

IZZY

He was a famous playwright who went to Harvard

MARTIN

So what?

IZZY

People care about that stuff Martin you have to stop being such a snob.

MARTIN

I'm a snob?

IZZY

You are a complete snob. Making fun of the way he talks

MARTIN

He talks like an idiot; his language is subhuman. It would be more interesting if it were subhuman then we could try and interpret what all the grunts and hand gestures mean, we could pretend he was a very clever chimpanzee who was teaching us how language actually worked but he doesn't do anything as interesting as that. He just says things, idiotic, meaningless, self important observations about nothing, his words have nothing behind them. There's no music there's no joy there's no curiosity there's nothing. And I'm not talking about a flat terrifying banality of evil nihilistic nothing, I'm talking about nothing.

IZZY

See that's what I mean. All this talk about language makes it sound like you don't like him.

KATE

You guys you have to stop talking about him.

IZZY

That's what I'm saying! Stop making such a big deal about 'language.'

MARTIN

I'm a writer we're all writers if we don't care about language what should we care about?

IZZY

Sex..

She leans in, suddenly lifts her shirt and shows him her tits. Martin reacts, startled but not uninterested.

KATE

IZZY!

MARTIN

Oh. Sex. Oh.

Laughing. Izzy does a little dance and falls back on the couch, throws her arms up in a pose.

IZZY

I'm going to write one of those drug menace books. You know all those old mass market paper backs that have the girls with their shirts off on the covers, all about smoking opium and ruining the lives of men. And then I'm going to pose for the cover and I'm going to be in New York magazine.

KATE

There's a career goal. Show your tits to New York Magazine.

IZZY

It's ironic and witty. I'm going to be famous.

She smiles at Martin, clearly flirtatious. Douglas reenters, oblivious. Izzy pulls her shirt down.

This place is great.

He sits.

What'd I miss?

Blackout.

Scene two

Lights up on Leonard, fifty, fierce and brilliant.

LEONARD

You got to understand that this is a totally irrelevant dream state you're hibernating in up here. It's irrelevant. I mean I was just in Moldova, doing research for this, thing and I ate cabbage with a Chechnyan psychopath. Then I'm in Dubai with a bunch of Shiites and Sunnis, people wanting to kill each other. I almost got into a fist fight with this Russian prostitute who was of a totally indeterminate gender, don't get me started on that story, anyway the fact is I was stoned out of my mind. It was fucked up, all of it, but it was relevant. The world we live in? It no longer exists! Last year I was in Rwanda. I was hanging out with this guy, he's a genocide survivor, his arms are gone, chopped off, he can't do anything anymore except beg for whatever pittance, half a bowl of rice some fucking UN peacekeeper throws him every other day, the rest of the time he just lies in the mud unless someone like me comes along and helps him get drunk. So I spend like three hours with this guy, listening to him tell his fucking story and finally he gets really quiet and he says, you know, he says listen man. I got HIV. I'm going to die. And I'm like forget it, I'm overwhelmed I go, why are you telling me all this? Why am I the receptacle of this incredible fucking story, man? And he says: Because you are a writer. You must write this. It must be told.
> (a beat)

How did I get off on this. What were we talking about?

MARTIN

Um, Kate had a story...

LEONARD

Right! Kate's story. Where is it?

MARTIN

It's in your hand.

Leonard finds it in his hand.

LEONARD
Yeah. Right. So what were we talking about?

KATE
The first sentence.

LEONARD
(reading)
Oh yeah, Christ, I remember now. Oh, Christ. "When truth is acknowledged universally it is also universally disdained." I mean what the fuck, I can't even—

KATE
That's not the whole sentence.

LEONARD
(abrupt)
Yeah I see that I see the semi-colon, I understand that that means there's only a partial stop and that more is coming but I'm not sure I want to continue. Okay? I'm not even making it through your first sentence. So why don't you tell me what you're doing because it's not exactly drawing me in here.

KATE
What am I—

LEONARD
What are you, yes, what are you doing?

KATE
(stumbling)
I'm it's a referencing of Jane Austen the first sentence of Pride and Prejudice, it's kind of a sardonic commentary.

LEONARD

What's so fucking sardonic about it?

KATE

It's the narrator she's

LEONARD

I don't give a shit about the narrator. If I can't get past the first five words how the fuck am I supposed to find out enough about the narrator to care about him?

KATE

It's not a him, it's a her.

LEONARD

Well see that would be my point. If I can't even tell what gender your narrator is, then you haven't really done your job have you?

KATE
(defending herself)
How if you don't go past the first five words how can you tell?

LEONARD

Listen to me. Don't defend yourself. If you're defending yourself you're not listening. I do know who your narrator is. She's an over-educated completely inexperienced sexually inadequate girl who has rich parents who give her everything and who has nothing to say, so she sits around and thinks about Jane Austen all the time. I don't give a shit about that person. This is what I'm saying. I don't have to go past the first five words because I already know enough and I don't give a shit.

IZZY

I liked it.

LEONARD

No you didn't.

IZZY

I did, I thought she was sort of doing this thing with sexual irony. Like the lack of sex was sort of like a come on.

DOUGLAS

I like it too. I think it's intelligent and thoughtful. Well done.

MARTIN

I like it too.

LEONARD

Guys! This is very sweet you're all adorable. But don't kid yourselves. You're all going to be nice to her now because her story tanked. But you're not in this together. And trust me, you wouldn't think the story was so great if it really were any good. If it were really good? You'd fucking hate it. Writers in their natural state are about as civilized as feral cats. All this 'well done' bullshit means you're not being honest and if you're not honest who gives a shit what you're writing. Who's up next.

He tosses Kate's story to the floor and looks around. There is a big old pause.

LEONARD

See you next week. Cowards.

He goes. They all sit there, silent for a moment.

IZZY

Oh god I can't believe how late it is! I have to go! My mom is in the hospital.

DOUGLAS

Wow that's a drag Izzy. You need a ride?

MARTIN

You drove to the upper west side?

DOUGLAS

No I meant on the subway.

MARTIN

You're going to give her a ride on the subway?

DOUGLAS

I just thought she maybe needed company. Her mom is in the hospital, Martin.

IZZY

It's not serious. I mean she's not dying or anything.

DOUGLAS

So you want to have a drink? Like on the way?

IZZY

Sure, great.

They go.

Martin looks at Kate.

MARTIN

You okay?

KATE

What do you think, MARTIN? Am I okay? AM I OKAY?

MARTIN

Sorry.

KATE

What an asshole. What a jerk.

MARTIN

Yeah.

KATE

People think he's a genius what is so fucking genius about that?

MARTIN

That is what I've been saying! 'Let me give you a ride home.' The guy's a moron.

KATE

Not Douglas, Martin! I'm talking about Leonard!. Leonard is an idiot!

MARTIN

Oh, I thought you were talking about Douglas.

KATE

Did you think that was smart? Did you think him standing there and telling us all that we're fucking losers if we don't go to Egypt and smoke water pipes, we're we're completely irrelevant as human beings if we read the New York Times, does that seem SMART to you?

MARTIN

That's not really what he said.

KATE

It is absolutely what he said! I'm irrelevant because I live in a nice apartment I love that. How about I'm irrelevant because I'm an overeducated girl—

MARTIN

That's not what he said.

KATE

He said I was sexually inadequate!

MARTIN

He said the story was sexually inadequate.

KATE

How would he know, he didn't read more than six words!

MARTIN

He's not talking about you, he's talking about the story.

KATE

A story he hasn't read.

MARTIN

He read the first page. I mean, we all sat here right, and watched him read the first page.

KATE

Big fucking deal! What is your point Martin?

MARTIN

I don't have a point! I just mean that's all we get right? Everybody says it. If you don't get them on the first page, that's all you get.

KATE

So it's my fault! That I stood here and got completely humiliated by that asshole?

She disappears into the apartment, yelling back. Martin waits.

KATE
(off)

Everybody acted like, they all said he's ROUGH but he's A GREAT TEACHER BUT I DON'T SEE WHAT'S SO GREAT ABOUT JUST BEING ABUSED. THAT'S NOT TEACHING THAT'S JUST BEING A SHITHEAD. IF I WANT SOMEONE TO TELL ME I'M WASTING MY TIME I CAN JUST TALK TO MY MOTHER. EVERYONE THINKS ITS SO COOL AND FUN TO BE MEAN TO ARTISTS BUT IF WE WEREN'T HERE THERE WOULD BE NOTHING BUT ANARCHY AND

IMMORALITY AND CHAOS. WE ARE THE SOUL OF THE
CULTURE AND PEOPLE CAN JUST FUCKING BE NICE TO
US ONCE IN A WHILE.

*She reappears, carrying bags of chips and diet soda and ice
cream. She sits down and starts to eat.*

MARTIN
What are you doing?

KATE
I'm depressed and I'm trying to make myself feel better is that all
right with you?

MARTIN
Don't be depressed.

KATE
My story got creamed. I'm depressed. I'm a depressed feral cat.

MARTIN
If you think he's stupid what do you care if he didn't like your story?

KATE
I didn't think he was stupid until he was stupid to me today.

MARTIN
So if he liked your story that would make him not stupid?

KATE
Yes! If he liked my story that would make him smart. Okay? Okay?
Okay?

MARTIN
Just wanted to be sure.

KATE

Why are you still here? Douglas is out there having drinks with the love of your life, why are you hanging out with the loser?

MARTIN

She's not the love of my life are you kidding?

KATE

Give me a break.

MARTIN

She's a twit!

KATE

Yeah, guys hate that. It sucks that she's gorgeous, too.

MARTIN

Look. She's all right. No, I mean, okay, she's attractive, no one is going to say she's not attractive.

He starts to eat, obsessively, everything in sight.

KATE

Oh my god you should hear yourself. 'Attractive.' Why don't you just put a gun to your own head, you're so completely in love with her. Do you think it's not utterly obvious to absolutely everyone who sees you in the same room with her?

MARTIN

I am not 'in love' with her. She's clearly got something going with Douglas. How she can even stand to talk to him for more than fifteen seconds at a go, is a mystery. The guy is an unmitigated embarrassment to the human race. Seriously. 'Can I give you a ride?' Give her a ride! It's so Darien. Maybe he could 'give her a ride' to Yaddo, where the interiority and the exteriority of the landscape is so stunningly in sync with the diasporic essentiality of the mimetic dialogue between self and culture. Maybe that's what he should do.

KATE

Don't kid yourself she would love a ride to Yaddo. Don't eat all the chips I want those.

MARTIN

Fuck me. Fuck her. Fuck him.

KATE

No fuck me! I'm the one who got creamed. This sucks. That story is fantastic. I have been working on that fucking story for six years, people love that story! You love that story.

MARTIN

Well.

KATE

What? What?

MARTIN

Nothing.

KATE

You don't love that story.

MARTIN

It's okay. You've been working on it for six years.

KATE

That's right I've been working on it for six years because people like it, people--Frank Conroy read it, before he died, he was the writer in residence up at Bennington for one month and he read that story and you know what he said to me? He said it was 'much better than most.' Not better than most. "Much" better than most.

MARTIN

'Much better than most,' that is so lame, Kate.

KATE

Yes, it would be lame, coming from you but it didn't come from you, it came from Frank Conroy. You know who else likes that story? Tobias Wolf. He read it when I took that summer writing class and he said it had some nice things in it.

MARTIN

Kate do you even hear yourself? You know how long you've been working on that story? Six years—

KATE

That's right, SIX YEARS.

MARTIN

Why have you been writing the same story for six years?

KATE

Because it's a good story! It's a really good story. When I was at Bennington—

MARTIN

Jesus, was there ever a time when you weren't at Bennington? You exist in an alternate universe called 'Bennington.'

KATE

I learned a lot there, Martin.

MARTIN

What you learned was how to write one lousy story in six years.

A silence.

MARTIN

That's not, I didn't mean the story was lousy.

KATE

Fuck you you did too.

MARTIN

Well why are you writing the same story for six years?

KATE

Because people kept telling me it was good but that it needed more work!

MARTIN

Well then Leonard just did you a big favor, didn't he?

A beat.

KATE

Meaning?

MARTIN

Now you can write something else.

A beat.

KATE

You know, this is my apartment, so I can't walk out. Could you walk out please?

MARTIN

No no, don't do that. Come on, don't do that.

KATE
(overlap)
I want to do that. Get out of my apartment. Get out. Go. Go. Get out.

MARTIN

No no no

KATE

I mean it, Martin--Martin--

MARTIN

Come on, listen to me. Listen.

He takes her hands. She looks away.

MARTIN

I have to tell you something.

She looks up at him. He holds her hand.

KATE

What?

MARTIN

I'm getting kicked out of my apartment because I'm a little late on
the rent. Can I stay here? I mean, you got like nine extra bedrooms.
And it's free! Who knew it was free? I can stay, right?

She looks at him.

Blackout.

Scene Three

Leonard is taking off his jacket and scarf, looking at the others, who are sitting dutifully around him.

LEONARD

So who's got something, who are we starting with today?

There is silence. No one moves. Leonard laughs.

LEONARD

Come on children we don't have all night. What are we here for? Am I a fucking writer, or am I a fucking piece of shit coward? Am I trying to construct a living breathing cosmos with language or am I just scratching on the wall of a cave? Am I feral cat or am I a useless goldfish in a bowl that would be better off someone flushed it down the toilet? Which is what's going to happen to it anyway.

Izzy twitches, nervous.

IZZY
(blurting)

I have something. I have a story. I didn't know if Douglas and Martin had something, I was thinking maybe they would want to go, or maybe Kate has something else—

KATE

No.

IZZY

Okay, well, I do have something.
(handing it over)
I haven't been working on it very long. I just started it. About a week a few days ago.

LEONARD

Yeah I can tell.

He holds it up; it's only two pages.

IZZY

Oh. Well but. Okay.

He starts to read as he talks.

LEONARD
No it's good, if you have something on the page you should let people see it for Christ's sake. All this rewriting people do, it squeezes the guts out of everything. I read this story last week, couple weeks ago, it was so fucking lifeless, this person had clearly been rewriting this stupid thing for maybe 10 years, there was just nothing left to it except a sort of desiccated corpse, it was ludicrous. If you're going to write, be a fucking man about it. Kerouac wrote On the Road in like a week or something.

KATE
Okay, I'm sorry but what did you say? Did you say you want us to 'be a fucking man' about writing, and that that we should write like Kerouac?

LEONARD
You should write like yourself.

KATE
Yes. Yes. I agree with that but if my 'self' is a woman, I don't see why I then should write like a man.

LEONARD
If you're going to be some fucking feminist about it, that would be up to you, but I can't help you with that.

KATE
Feminist, I didn't say feminist, I said woman. Woman. What is wrong with being a woman and being a writer.

LEONARD

You would have to answer that for yourself.

KATE

But you said it. You said, 'be a man,' be Jack Kerouac who was a total pig to women—

LEONARD

Look, you want to argue about feminist politics, I'm not here to argue with you about that. I'm here to talk about writing.

KATE

But we're not talking about writing—

LEONARD

Well, no because you've commandeered the conversation. Is it all right with you if we talk about the story your fellow writer has presented to the group?

KATE

Sure. Of course. Sure.

> *There is a moment of silence while Leonard reads. He laughs at something. Izzy smiles. As Leonard keeps laughing, Izzy is more and more pleased.*

LEONARD

Well, this is.... It's fresh. It's lively as hell. Do you have copies?

IZZY

(happy)

Yes, yes I do.

LEONARD

Okay, pass them out because people should, we'll talk about this one. There is real energy here. A lightness, a touch, a sexual edge to the language which is I got to say, it got me on board. Va voom.

Like, this thing I read last week--I don't remember when I read it--it was like a lump of nothing, there was no forward motion, it just laid there, the words were like lumps of shit—

KATE

Hey. HEY. Could you, I mean, I just, that's--if you don't—

LEONARD

Look, what is your problem? I am trying to teach a class here!

KATE

You're not teaching, you're just insulting--me--you're just—

LEONARD

I'm not insulting anybody I'm telling your fellow writer--what's your name again?

IZZY

Izzy.

LEONARD

I'm telling Izzy about the experience of reading her story! Which you know you might want to participate in. But, if you can't support your fellow writer, that would be up to you.

KATE

Look, this is—

MARTIN

Maybe if we continued to talk about Izzy's story—

LEONARD

That's what I'm trying to do—

MARTIN

Without--I think what Kate is getting hung up on is that you keep insulting her work.

LEONARD

This isn't about her!

MARTIN

Yes. That's right. But it's hard, because you keep bringing up that story, from last week—

LEONARD

That's got nothing to do with her!

MARTIN

Well, it was her story, so—

LEONARD

That wasn't her story!

MARTIN

It wasn't?

KATE

It wasn't?

LEONARD

No, Christ! That was a totally different situation, that's what I'm saying! That was somebody else's story, this relentlessly talent-free story about some girl who had this obsession with Jane Austen, Christ what a soul-sucking waste of words that was.

MARTIN

That was Kate's story.

LEONARD

That was your story?

KATE

Yes, that was my story.

LEONARD
Oh. Oh! That was your story.

KATE
Yes.

LEONARD
Oh. Okay. Sorry. You know. Obviously I didn't think that story really worked. But this, you know... who wrote this?

IZZY
I did.

LEONARD
This has a great, you know, really great sexual feel to it.

IZZY
Thank you.

LEONARD
The tone of Asian exoticism, it's good. I was in Shanghai once, have you been to Shanghai?

IZZY
I have an uncle who lives there.

LEONARD
I bet you do.

DOUGLAS
Can we talk about the story? I just have some questions. Because I admire it, I really do Izzy, there's a terrific tone that's both sinister and wry, that I think is truly original but I'm actually a little unsure where, of course not that with two pages you'd have to have the whole thing planned out but I'm more or less curious—

LEONARD

Where? Who gives a shit where. Why would you ask that question at this point, don't ask where, when 'where' is the point, am I right?

He looks at Izzy, who has the good grace to be confused.

IZZY

Well, it's just really new. I think 'where' is a good question. That's why I wasn't sure I should even show it to you. Because 'where'—

LEONARD

I'm not saying 'where' is not a good question. But that's what I admire about the energy of the opening. It dares to ask that question and not know the answer. The writing itself is asking the question. See, this reminds me, when I was at Yale with Penn Warren, there was no getting past him, no point even trying. He was ruthless and religious about sound. Everything else, intellect, idea, motion, character, all were secondary, if the sound wasn't there, there was no discussion even capable of continuing in a meaningful--I'm not saying this right. No. I am, actually. I am. This has a sound. It rings like a bell. It doesn't matter that there's no subject or story or idea or meaning. It's got power. It's got sex. Well done. Well done. What's your name?

IZZY

Izzy.

LEONARD

Well done, Izzy. What else have you got?

He sits next to her on the couch. The intentions of his attention are clear. She looks at him, smiles.

Blackout.

Scene Four

It is later the same night. Martin sits on the side of the couch, drinking a beer, watching Kate move in and out of the room with a bowl of cookie dough. She holds it and mixes it with a blender. The plug pulls out of the wall in the next room. She goes back and plugs it in, then reenters with the whirling mixer.

KATE

Two pages. It wasn't even two pages. It was a page and a half!

MARTIN

It's more than a page and a half.

KATE

It's not two pages.

MARTIN

It's almost two pages.

KATE

What can you fucking tell from two fucking pages?

MARTIN

Two good pages?

KATE

They're not good! How can you say they're good! You don't honestly think those two idiotic pages are good!

MARTIN

They're not bad, Kate—

KATE

They're horrible! Oh my god do you honestly think that shit is good?

I think—

KATE

You just want to sleep with her, you don't know what you think. I can't believe it.

He watches her eat a big spoon of cookie dough.

MARTIN

What are you doing?

KATE

I'm eating cookie dough.

MARTIN

I can't believe girls actually do that. Girls actually do that.

KATE

I can't believe that men think that because they maybe want to sleep with someone that means she's a good writer. That is what I can't believe.

Martin starts to eat the cookie dough with her.

MARTIN

She is a good writer.

KATE

I am a good writer, Martin! Just because none of you want to sleep with me, that doesn't mean I'm not any good! Let me tell you something, if this writing seminar were made up of exclusively lesbian writers, I'd be a fucking star.

MARTIN

Are you a lesbian?

                              KATE

Martin! You know I'm not a lesbian!

                            MARTIN

People change their minds.

                              KATE

Well, I have not changed my mind. I'm just a lonely bad writer who's getting fat.

                            MARTIN

Shit. This stuff is delicious.

                    They fight over the bowl.

                            MARTIN

Listen. You are totally hot. You don't need a bunch of lesbians to tell you that.

                              KATE

Izzy is hot.

                            MARTIN

You're hot too. I often go to bed thinking about you in the bath tub with Jack Kerouac. That turned out to be a very potent image for me. "Jack, Jack, Jack--"

                              KATE

Oh that's the thumping I've been hearing, down the hall.

                            MARTIN

"Jack, Jack, Jack--"

                              KATE

Give me that--

            Laughing, she climbs on top of him. There is a moment

which gets just a shred too close. The door buzzes. The buzzer continues, insistent. The moment evaporates. She goes to the wall and hits it.

MARTIN

What's that?

KATE

Chinese food.

MARTIN

You ordered chinese food?

KATE

Yes I did. I'm a terrible writer and I am I am committed to getting fat. It's a commitment now.

MARTIN

Kate I think your story was really good.

KATE

You do not. Leonard hated it so much that within one week it's become legendary in his imagination, how bad it was. And now I'm stuck here. I'm stuck here with that asshole in my apartment for TEN WEEKS. I suck. My life has no meaning.

MARTIN

Your life has meaning.

KATE

No it doesn't and yours doesn't either.

MARTIN

My life has meaning.

KATE

Please. It does not. On top of which you're afraid that the girl you're crushing on—

MARTIN

I'm not crushing on Izzy—

KATE

It doesn't matter if you are or not because she has other fish to fry, doesn't she, she's not afraid to show off her writing, and she's going to get it published too because Izzy is not afraid of doing whatever she has to and right now she is off having sex with our hideous and disgusting teacher.

MARTIN

Izzy is not-having sex with Leonard. That would be completely unethical.

KATE

Which is why of course it would never happen.

He opens another bottle. There is a knock at the door. Kate answers it.

Hi Douglas, what are you doing here?

He barges in and sits. Martin stares at him.

DOUGLAS

She's having sex with him! It's completely unethical. I mean, I wouldn't care, it's not like I'm a prude god knows.

MARTIN

Izzy's not having sex with Leonard.

DOUGLAS

They went home together!

MARTIN

You don't know that!

DOUGLAS

Martin. We left the apartment and went to that shitty bar across the street to have a drink. After three glasses of wine each, he looked her in the face and said, you want to come back to my place? And she said sure. And they left. Together.

MARTIN

That doesn't mean she slept with him.

DOUGLAS

They were making out on the sidewalk in front of the restaurant! Right in front of me. The table is here. The plate glass window is here. And they start making out right here. If the window hadn't been there, they would have been in my lap. He was feeling her up right in front of me.

MARTIN

Come on.

DOUGLAS

Do you think I'd make something like that up?

MARTIN

Well what was she doing?

DOUGLAS

She was participating!

MARTIN

That is so unethical. For Leonard to take advantage of her like that.

KATE

You are insane.

MARTIN

You don't think it's unethical.

KATE

I think that Izzy is going to get her story published in the New Yorker is what I think.

DOUGLAS

You can't get your work published by sleeping with your fiction teacher, Kate.

KATE

I'm sorry what did you say?

DOUGLAS

I just don't think that Izzy is naive enough to think that sleeping with Leonard will help her career.

KATE

Naive? You think it's 'naive' of her to think something like that?

DOUGLAS

I think I know a little bit more about it than you do.

KATE

Oh that was helpful.

DOUGLAS

I just meant.

KATE

I know what you meant. Here's what I meant: Calling a woman or a man who sleeps with a powerful guy naive, is naive.

DOUGLAS

Which is still unethical. It just makes Leonard's behavior coercive.

KATE

Coercive! Maybe it was coercive of Izzy to write two pages of a story that's all about sex and then go have drinks with her fucked up writing teacher who can't remember anybody's name because he's constantly thinking about his dick. Maybe that was the coercive part.

DOUGLAS

And maybe you're jealous.

KATE

Maybe I'm jealous? Maybe you're an idiot—

DOUGLAS

Maybe I'm an idiot? Maybe—

MARTIN

SHUT UP! Would both of you just--shut up? Please. Just shut up.

Really sad and depressed, Martin takes another bottle of beer, looks at them, tries to speak, can't, and goes.

Buzzer.

DOUGLAS

What's that?

KATE

Chinese food.

Blackout.

Scene Five

Leonard is looking at some pages. All four sit and watch him. Leonard paces. He finishes reading a page, drops it to the ground. He reads another page, paces. Drops it to the ground. He starts to read another page. It is excruciating. Finally he glances through the other pages, looks up at Douglas.

LEONARD
Your uncle said you were talented.

DOUGLAS
Oh, thank you. That's really nice of you to say.

LEONARD
I didn't say you were talented. I said, your UNCLE said you were talented.
(then)
I didn't say you weren't talented. This is not without talent. This section about the top of the girl's dresser, the two bottles of fingernail polish standing next to each other like "lost and terrified soldiers," that's not bad. It's nice that you've already referenced the peeling of the red polish on her toes, so we get the allusion to blood without having stated it explicitly. It's all right. Good, even. Your description of the butterfly poster over the bed is first rate. It's not the pedestrian interpretation one might be tempted to make about teenage girls and butterflies. "There was a time when tribal peoples had carved butterflies into stone, had reckoned them messengers from the gods." Those tribal peoples are fantastic, the way you drop them in, it's a beautiful surprise. You paint her bedroom well.

DOUGLAS
Thank you.

MARTIN
Wow. A teenage girl's bedroom. Wow.

You don't like it?

No, it's terrific. Well done.

LEONARD
No, go ahead.

MARTIN
I like it. I'm a little confused about the relevance factor, just two weeks ago you told us all we should be writing about dying beggars in the Sudan, so I'm not without confusion now, how this does that, but it's not without talent. That's what I always said about Douglas, he's not without talent.

LEONARD
Don't be such a pussy.

MARTIN
A pussy.

LEONARD
You don't think you're being a pussy?

MARTIN
Do I think I'm being a pussy?

IZZY
Martin.

MARTIN
'Martin,' what? Do you like it?

IZZY
I do, yeah, I like it a lot.

MARTIN

Do you think I'm being a pussy?

KATE

I think it's a pretty good story, too. It's good, Douglas.

MARTIN

Oh it's a 'pretty good story' and I'm a pussy, that's great. I thought this was a writing seminar where we discussed, um, 'writing' with something approaching intellectual sophistication. "Pretty good story" and I'm a "pussy." We're ascending the heights here.

LEONARD

I think the word "pussy" is pretty intellectually sophisticated. It communicates pretty precisely the meaning I'm looking for.

MARTIN

My point--my point is –

LEONARD

I know your point. You don't like me calling you a pussy, even though you're acting like a pussy, because you're here to discuss the writing, you guys are all paying me a lot of money, because you think I can help you understand the craft of writing better, so that you can go off and have successful so-called careers, as writers of fiction, which is more or less my specialty. Or is something else your problem.

He is standing behind Izzy. He puts his hand on her hair and strokes it, once. Martin looks at them both.

MARTIN

No, that's pretty much my problem. I'm here to talk about writing, I'd like to do that without the word pussy being involved unless that's a big problem for you.

LEONARD
(a beat)
No, I think I can handle that.

MARTIN
Thank you.

LEONARD
So why don't you tell us what you think about the story. Since you want to stay focused on the writing, and you don't think you're a pussy, I think we'd all like to hear what you have to say about today's writing specimen, offered up to us with friendly, indeed almost dog-like equanimity, by our not untalented friend, Douglas. Douglas your uncle mentioned that the New Yorker is seriously looking at one of your stories, is that this one?

DOUGLAS
Yes, I, yes it is, it is actually.

LEONARD
Why don't you tell us what you think about that, Martin.

There is a pause.

DOUGLAS
Look—

LEONARD
You stay out of this. Come on, Martin! Tell your fellow writer--the one person in the room who is in fact succeeding at something you are failing at--tell him what you think. And tell the truth. Come on! Come on!

MARTIN
All right—

IZZY
Well I love it. Seriously, the language is amazing, Douglas. I just learned a ton from it. And frankly, I know that Martin thinks so too. He told me last week! We both read your other story, the one in Tin House and Martin flipped.

LEONARD
Did he?

IZZY
Yes he did. He thinks Douglas is a thrilling writer. That's what he told me at least.

MARTIN
Yeah, I like Douglas's work a lot.

KATE
I like it too, Douglas. It's good.

DOUGLAS
Thanks Izzy. Thanks Kate. Thanks Martin.

They all sit in silence for a moment, while Leonard laughs a little, shakes his head.

LEONARD
You guys are hilarious. All right. Good for you, Martin, that Izzy managed to tell us all how much you liked Douglas's writing before you told him it sucked. Because that would have been awkward.

MARTIN
It doesn't suck, it's good.

LEONARD
Yes, it is good. There's a level of competence here that is almost chilling in its thoroughness. This is the perfection rendition of a New Yorker story. Capable, graceful in places, a detached tone of

perplexed intelligence, you have a relatively famous last name, in literary circles, not too famous but famous enough. It's not a home run but it's a standing double.

He hands it back to Douglas.

DOUGLAS
Well but I'd really like to hear some criticism.

LEONARD
Oh you'd like that.

DOUGLAS
I would! I'd love to build on what's here. See if I can mine the interiority of the Stephanie character especially, I feel like she's just, there's a few places where the complexity of her need for emotional distance is maybe not fully rendered.

LEONARD
Yeah that's the problem with emotionally distant characters, it's hard to write about them because who gives a shit finally about someone who's got no interior life.

DOUGLAS
No I don't think she has no interior life, that's not—

LEONARD
All right. I'm going to level with you. I'm going to give you some advice here that I think is going to be totally like on the money useful to you.

DOUGLAS
Great.

LEONARD
It's going to sound a little rough but you expect that, yeah? I mean, you're not going to turn into a big baby about the truth unlike some

other people?

DOUGLAS

No. Of course not.

LEONARD

Good. Because there is something in your writing--it's hard to, it's around the tonal perfection, there's a kind of--its a little like a whore.

DOUGLAS

The character of Stephanie?

LEONARD

No no not the character. You. The way you talk about writing is kind of stupid. Plus, the way you write is so unimaginative in the way it attacks the problem you set yourself. I mean, it's skillful, but whorish. It's like the way you play your name off, your connections, you're a name dropper, you're a whore. And that's in the writing. It's perfect, in a kind of whorish way. I don't know why you're wasting your time on fiction. I mean, you're good at it, I'm not saying you're not.

DOUGLAS

No. Oh! No.

LEONARD

It's just--if you can do this? Why not make a ton of money doing this. You're capable, you've got a few publications under your belt, a famous last name, they love that shit in Hollywood. You could make a fuckload of money. Or you could spend the rest of your life writing fiction that nobody reads or respects, even if they read it. Cause you're talented, like I said, but you're never going to be great. And there are a lot of people who are never going to be great, most fiction writers just evaporate, really, but that's going to be a problem for you because of your kind of whorish attitude to the whole thing, the name dropping, and of course the name. It will in fact be particularly degrading and even humiliating to be ignored to the degree you will be ignored. Because at the same time you'll be allowed in, because of the name. You'll be invited to cocktail parties. You'll get to go to exclusive events at the Public Library. But you will never be on a panel. Because too many people who know shit will know: It's hollow. The work is hollow. I'd think about Hollywood.

DOUGLAS

Oh.

MARTIN

Yeah but... the story is excellent.

LEONARD

Yes we've all heard that you think the story is thrilling. I don't think it's thrilling. I think it's good, in a whorish way, and that that is the level of his writing ambition, and that he could make a fuckload of money in Hollywood.

DOUGLAS

But I, I'm a fiction writer.

LEONARD

You asked for the truth. That's the truth I have.

DOUGLAS

Yes. No. Thanks.

LEONARD

All right then. I got to go to Somalia tomorrow so I'll see you pussies in two weeks.

And he goes. There is a long moment of silence.

KATE

He's going to Somalia. Maybe someone will shoot him.

MARTIN

I think it's a really good story.

DOUGLAS

Fuck you. You think it's shit. At least he told me what he really thinks.

(then)

Could someone check in the hallway and make sure that he's gone?

KATE

Sure.

She opens the door, goes out, looks down the stairs. Comes back in.

KATE

He's gone.

DOUGLAS

Good.

He goes.

KATE

Douglas, wait. Don't just go walking off, Douglas wait!

Kate goes after him, leaving the door standing open. Martin sits on the couch, morose. Izzy turns back to him.

IZZY

You're an asshole.

MARTIN

I'm an asshole? HE'S an asshole! Not Douglas. Leonard. I think Douglas is a shit writer, but he's not an asshole. He's not actually a shit writer, either. He's a pretty good writer, who mostly writes shit.

IZZY

Which is what Leonard said.

MARTIN

Are you siding with Leonard now?

IZZY

I'm not siding with anyone, this is a situation! What is the matter with you?

MARTIN

What is the matter with ME?

IZZY

You were about to tell Douglas his story sucked—

MARTIN

I—

IZZY

You were too, and I saved you, you jerk. Douglas is hooked up and P.S. he's a good guy, you need to make him your friend. You want to keep getting rejected by Yaddo and McDowell, why don't you just keep sending blind submissions to those places like every other loser in the world.

MARTIN

Hey! Don't hold back.

IZZY

I'm not because you know what? I don't care what anyone says, we're in this together and it's a game, it's a situation, and we need each other. Douglas can help us. Leonard too.

MARTIN

Fuck Leonard. That guy is an ASSHOLE. Everybody was like 'oh he's amazing, he only takes a few students anymore, you'll learn so much.' This is what I'm learning: GIVE ME MY MONEY BACK. I can't BELIEVE I scraped together five thousand dollars for this. I can't even pay my rent.

IZZY

Maybe the reason you're not learning anything Martin is that you haven't shown him any of your work, has that occurred to you?

MARTIN

Well maybe I don't want to show him my work because all I've seen him do for my fellow writers is stomp on their hearts or call them whores or turn them into whores.

A beat.

MARTIN

Sorry.

IZZY

You mistake me, Martin, for someone who gives a shit what you think.

MARTIN

Yes. I see your point there. You, clearly, you should go ahead and do whatever you think you need to do.

IZZY

Just for the record, however, I did not sleep with Leonard.

MARTIN

It's none of my business. You're right.

IZZY

I didn't sleep with him! Don't you believe me?

MARTIN

It doesn't matter if I believe you or not, Izzy, it's none of my business—

IZZY

Are you calling me a liar now? Now I'm not just a whore, I'm a liar and a whore?

MARTIN

I didn't say that!

IZZY

Douglas is right. At least Leonard tells the truth.

She goes and gets her purse, to go.

MARTIN

Look, why are you mad at me? You're right! I'm pathetic, I'm a
pathetic--chicken--but I just, I think that you could do a lot better
than that, that-- You're so beautiful, Izzy, you're exquisite, really, just--
funny and smart and so full of life—

IZZY

Am I?

MARTIN

Well...yeah.

IZZY

You're right. Since I'm not sleeping with him, I could surely do a lot
better.

MARTIN

Well, you could.

IZZY

Could I?

MARTIN

Well yeah.

She starts to move toward him.

IZZY

How much better?

MARTIN

Well...a lot. Really a whole lot. A lot.

She is close. She kisses him. And kisses him again. He participates.

IZZY

You know what, Martin? I think you're right. Where's your bedroom?

MARTIN

Where's--

IZZY

The bedroom. The bedroom, Martin. The bedroom.

He finally comes to his senses and takes her off to his bedroom. There is a moment of silence. Finally, Kate steps inside the open door from the hallway, where she has witnesses the whole scene. She leans against the door, closing it behind her. After a moment, alone, she starts to cry.

Blackout.

Scene Six

Two weeks later. Douglas on the couch. He is reading a manuscript.

DOUGLAS

Kate, get out here. Kate. What is this?

Kate enters.

KATE

Do you like it?

DOUGLAS

It's interesting. Who wrote it?

KATE

This friend of mine.

DOUGLAS

Is it true?

KATE

He says it is.

DOUGLAS

A transvestite Cubano gang leader.

KATE

He's pretty extreme, yes.

DOUGLAS

Do you believe it?

KATE

Do I believe it's true?

DOUGLAS

Yeah.

KATE

Well, I knew him at Bennington.

DOUGLAS

So that makes it by default what, true or false?

KATE

I don't know. I thought he was pretty good. The teachers all loved him because he had this exotic Cubano past.

DOUGLAS

How'd he even get there? To Bennington?

KATE

I don't know. Some adult ed prison program.

DOUGLAS

I thought you knew this guy.

KATE

I do know him, he lives in the village. I bumped into him in a coffee shop last week and he told me what he was writing so I said could I see it and... that's what he gave me.

DOUGLAS

He had it on him.

KATE

Yes he had it on him. Like you, apparently, he has a whorish essence. He'll give it up to anybody.

DOUGLAS

So why am I reading this?

KATE

I'm going to show it to fuckface.

DOUGLAS

Why?

There is the sound of laughter, then Martin.

MARTIN
(off)

Give it to me. Oh my god this is no joke Izzy come on--

Izzy, in a man's shirt and underwear, runs into the room, laughing, holding several pages. Martin grabs her from behind, and they wrestle, laughing as she tries to keep the pages from him. They finally fall against the wall, making out. The kissing keeps going to the extent that it is not clear that they are aware that Douglas and Kate are in the room.

KATE
(to Douglas)

One would say 'get a room' but they have a room. It's a huge apartment, they could have six rooms if they wanted. But they seem to like it out here.
(yelling)

HEY. MARTIN. IZZY. WE ARE NOT IN FACT MAKING PORNO VIDEOS OUT HERE. COULD YOU TAKE THIS ELSEWHERE?

Martin pulls away, flustered.

MARTIN

Oh. Sorry. Sorry. Come on, Izzy. Come on. Hi Douglas.

Izzy is laughing. She allows herself to be pulled back to the bedroom.

DOUGLAS
How long has that been going on?

KATE
Two weeks. The night Leonard told you you were a whore, they both felt so bad for you they needed to comfort each other.

DOUGLAS
That's been going on for two weeks?

KATE
Yes.

DOUGLAS
Really.

KATE
Yes. In addition to looking like that, Izzy is apparently, in truth, a total nymphomaniac. Which was, shall we say, good news for Martin.

DOUGLAS
And they're staying here?

KATE
(An explosion of frustration)
I said he could live here! He didn't have a place to live! And she still lives at home with her parents, so that's out!

DOUGLAS
Yeah, but...

KATE
I'm not going to tell them they have to leave. They're happy, why would I resent the fact that they're happy. Leonard's been gone for two weeks, no one is having their hearts stomped on, and there are two happy people in love in my apartment. Why would I be

anything except happy happy happy myself. I'm so fucking happy.

She is clearly not. Douglas looks at her.

KATE

Is that all you're going to read?

DOUGLAS

I just don't know why you want me to read it.

KATE

I want to quit the group. Luis said he would love to meet Leonard, he thinks Leonard might be able to do something for him. So I offered to sell him the last half of the sessions. I could get twenty five hundred bucks back and maybe go somewhere, I don't much give a shit where, just somewhere else, Ohio is looking pretty fucking good right now, just get away from this until I get a clue. About what I maybe should be doing with my life.

DOUGLAS
(with compassion)

Katie...

KATE

Don't be nice to me. I'm doing this and I'm not going to know you anymore.

DOUGLAS

Okay. Fine. But, you know, if you want to get away from all this--
this is your apartment.

KATE

It's my father's apartment.

DOUGLAS

My point being, if you want this to be over, you could just kick us all out.

KATE

Yes, I realize that. And I honestly think that slinking off like a dying cat would be better.

There is a knock at the door.

KATE

Oh goody, that would be Leonard! How splendid.

She opens the door. Leonard saunters in, fresh from the jungle.

KATE

Hey, Leonard. How was Somalia.

LEONARD

Didn't get shot. What a fucking country. It's just total chaos. I mean serious anarchic shit. Everywhere.

KATE

Sounds wonderful.

LEONARD

It was fucked! An entire people--erased--you look in their eyes and they laugh and smile and there is nothing there! An entire nation of sociopaths. Eight year old kids roaming the streets with AK 47s. Warlords sitting like kings on top of huge mounds of food, they use the bags of rice and beans and corn meal, they use it for their thrones. They sit up there and laugh at the people, their own people starving all around them. You sit on top of the food, you get a great view of it all, apparently.

DOUGLAS

It sounds amazing. You going to write about it?

LEONARD

You know -listen to me. Listen. You should go. Honestly, Douglas,

you should get yourself on a fucking cargo ship and go over there
and take a look at it. There are no embassies, no protections, there's
no one there who's responsible. Get yourself kidnapped, held at
gunpoint by pirates. Fuck them, they don't think you can write.
You go over there, you spend a few years facing the most terrifying
nihilism this planet has to offer, no one will dismiss you then.

KATE
Actually Leonard aside from you, no one is dismissing him.

LEONARD
He knows what I'm talking about.

KATE
Go get yourself shot by sociopaths, that will make you a writer. What
responsible advice.

LEONARD
Trust me, there's worse advice out there. I could have told you
to keep writing that fucking shitty story. Other people would've.
Where's the other two. Am I early?

KATE
MARTIN! IZZY! LEONARD's here! We're ready to start!

> There is an awkward moment while Leonard tries to figure
> out what is up. He looks around at Douglas, who shrugs.
> He looks down at the manuscript on the table, sits in front
> of it.

KATE
That's from a friend of mine. He's interested in joining the group.

LEONARD
I'm not taking extra students right now, I only take a few at a time,
tell him he can submit through a teacher like everyone else.

He holds it up. She doesn't take it.

KATE

He, I'm leaving the group. He's really good. We thought, he has a really fucked up story, he used to be in a Cubano gang, in high school, and he's actually a cross dresser. This is true. It's completely the kind of thing I think that you're looking for and I'm not--I'm not interested so much. As I thought I was. In being a writer.

He sets it down, looks at her.

LEONARD
                      (Cold)

I give a shit.

KATE

No, that's what I'm saying.

LEONARD

Boo hoo, someone has decided not to be a writer. No ones cares. No one in New York, no one in America, no one in Somalia--trust me. No one cares.

KATE

I'm well aware. That's why I'm quitting.

LEONARD

I'm not giving you your money back.

KATE
                    (starting to lose it)

Yes I'm AWARE. I am not asking you for my money back!

LEONARD

It's not your money. You paid me for my time. I am here, I show up every week. If that's not enough for you—

KATE

I didn't, that's not--
                    (to Douglas)
See? See? I can't even--I'm trying to slink off like a dying fucking animal and I can't even—

LEONARD

Slink off then! Why are you still here?

KATE
                    (loud)
BECAUSE IT'S MY APARTMENT.

LEONARD

Fuck you, we'll find someplace else to meet.

KATE

I just want to leave.

LEONARD

So GO. You're a weenie, you're a whiner, you can't take the merest shred of criticism—

KATE

That was not, what you said about my story was not—

LEONARD

The fucking critics will say worse. To all of you. If it gets in. If it gets in, at all, you're doomed.

> *There is a sad moment at this. Martin and Izzy come out from the other room. Both are fully dressed and pretending that they were not, mere moments ago, screwing their brains out.*

MARTIN

Hey. What's going on?

LEONARD

Nothing. Just a delightful welcome home from the scariest fucking trip of my life. Kate here was just telling me how happy she is to see me. Almost got shot twice. Didn't quite get a chance to tell that story, she had a lot of whining to do, I'm not nice enough.

KATE

That's not... Oh, god. That's not. This isn't....

LEONARD

Forget it.

He sits and reads the manuscript on the table. They watch him, glance at each other. No one knows what to do. After a moment, Leonard starts to laugh, lightly. The writing students look at each other. He laughs again, nods. He turns the page. Everyone watches each other, and him, while he reads.

LEONARD
(pleased)

Shit. Shit!

KATE

You like it. You think it's good?

He doesn't look up, keeps reading.

MARTIN

What's he reading?

LEONARD

What's this guy's name?

KATE

Luis.

LEONARD

Get him in here.

He keeps reading.

Blackout.

Scene Seven

Later that night. Leonard is gone. They are having beers.

MARTIN
(Mad)
Who is this guy?

KATE
I told you, Martin! He's this guy I knew from Bennington and I know you think that Bennington is some sort of crazy Vermont hippie commune where people get stoned all the time and no one can actually write—

MARTIN
I never said that—

KATE
You so did and I don't care, I'm just telling you, this guy was at Bennington when I was there and he's a good writer and I don't want to do it anymore so he's going to take my spot. I need the money. I'm going to Ohio.

MARTIN
You're going where?

KATE
I'M GOING TO OHIO. I'M GOING TO OHIO.

MARTIN
Why?

KATE
What do you care?

MARTIN
(reaching out to touch her shoulder)

What is that supposed to mean? Of course I care. Kate.

KATE

Do not, please do not—

DOUGLAS

Leave it alone, would you Martin?

MARTIN

Leave what alone? She's leaving! I'm just I'm catching up. You're leaving?

KATE
(hissing)
Yes. I'm leaving.

She leaves.

MARTIN
(to Douglas)
What is going on?

DOUGLAS

You're a total moron, is what is going on.

IZZY

So it's really good, huh?

DOUGLAS
(a beat)
I read a couple pages. It was good.

MARTIN

It's good?

DOUGLAS

I only read a few pages.

IZZY

Leonard seemed to like it. Like he just sat there. And kept reading it.

MARTIN

Yes, we all saw him Izzy.

IZZY

Do not snap at me. I have been fucking you for two weeks as you have never been fucked in your life, you are not allowed to snap at me!

MARTIN

I wasn't snapping.

IZZY

You were, definitely snapping, because you're worried.

MARTIN

What would I be worried about?

IZZY

You're worried about this new guy, who might be good.

MARTIN

(yelling)

KATE! Hey KATE!

Kate reenters, pouring herself a glass of white wine.

KATE

(Annoyed now)

What?

MARTIN

So you've read it, this guy's story.

KATE

It's not a story, it's a memoir.

MARTIN

And it's good?

KATE

I liked it. I think he's a really good writer, and he's kind of cracked, he wears dresses you have to put up with that, but he's nice and he has an interesting history and he can write!

DOUGLAS

So you think it's good.

KATE

I think it's good. I think it's really really good.

There is a pause at this.

MARTIN

You fucker.

KATE

What?

MARTIN

You wrote it.

KATE

Yes I did and Leonard loved it. Fucker. Stupid fucking mother fucker. A Cubano transvestite gang member. And he loved it! Asshole.

DOUGLAS

You wrote it?

KATE

Of course I wrote it! His biggest objection to me is that I'm a rich white girl. Maybe if I'm not a rich white girl we can find out if I can write.

> *Izzy starts to laugh. They are both laughing. Martin doesn't get it.*

DOUGLAS

Okay fine. You tricked us all, that's hilarious. But what are you going to do now?

KATE

What do you mean, what am I going to do? I'm on a roll! I'm going to keep writing!

DOUGLAS

Yeah, but you can't publish it.

KATE

Why not? Leonard loves it. He loves it more than he's loved anything that anyone has handed in so far.

IZZY

He liked my story.

KATE

He wanted to sleep with you.

IZZY

He wouldn't have if he didn't like the story.

MARTIN

You can't publish that as a memoir.

KATE

People do it all the time.

MARTIN

And they get arrested for it.

KATE

Nobody gets arrested for it! You get put on talk shows for it.

MARTIN

It's a lie!

KATE

It's fiction, I wrote a piece of fiction.

DOUGLAS

You said it was a memoir.

KATE

That's part of the fiction.

MARTIN

Don't even. Fiction is fiction. Art is art. The kind of truth that fiction is is is beyond these kinds of games, which is why you get PILLORIED for it, which is how by the way those people who do it get on talk shows, the only way to answer that kind of behavior is a complete public SHAMING. Saying a lie is the truth is a lie. And it's the kind of lie that sets a bomb off in your soul. And then you're fucked.

IZZY

Wow.

MARTIN

It is! What you write is like Douglas's butterflies, a messenger from the Gods--

DOUGLAS

Really?

MARTIN

Yes! A messenger from the gods, which has to be reckoned with! Or you're fucked!

KATE

Martin, you don't get to vote! You don't have enough money to pay your own rent! You're such a huge fucking chicken about your own work, you won't even show it! If it's a fucking message then what's the message? Oops! No one knows! Because you're a writer who no one can read! So you don't get a vote!

A beat.

KATE

Well done, Kate! You not only pulled one over on Leonard who everyone in the room thinks is a flaming abusive BUTTHOLE, you came up with a terrific piece of writing! We know you've been feeling shitty about yourself because of the way Leonard treated you and you've been really nice to let Martin and Izzy use your apartment as a FUCKING LOVE NEST and well done well done you must feel a lot better, that piece you wrote about the Cubano transvestite gang member is really smart and edgy and funny, you're a writer after all. Well done.
(then, playing her part)
Thanks, thanks you guys. Thanks!

She drinks. Douglas laughs. Then he laughs some more.

KATE

Thank you, Douglas. At least somebody appreciates the effort.

DOUGLAS

No, you're right. You're absolutely right! It's no worse than what Leonard did. It's practically the exact same thing.

MARTIN

Oh yeah? On top of everything else he publishes phony memoirs?

DOUGLAS

Worse. I was really upset after Leonard called me a whore last
week so I called my uncle to talk to him about it? And he told me.
Leonard's no saint.

KATE

Who thought he was a saint?

IZZY

Your uncle dished dirt on Leonard?

DOUGLAS

Yes, he did.

MARTIN

So spill it. What'd Leonard do?

DOUGLAS

                    (a beat)
He's a plagiarist.

IZZY

Get out.

MARTIN

You're kidding.

KATE

Are you sure?

DOUGLAS

There was some incident, it got totally hushed up. But that's why
Leonard stopped publishing. This was like an ice age ago, but he
did, he totally plagiarized something, it was from like a student,
and it wrecked his career. After those first few novels he was done.
And then I don't know what happened, but eventually someone at
Random House took pity on him and threw him a copy editing gig

and he turned out to be this rock star editor, and then he started doing all those magazine pieces on Africa and after a while people just forgot about it. Nobody really cares now, but it was apparently a big deal when it happened.

MARTIN

Okay wait. I just have to ask you something. Hearing that your writing teacher is a plagiarist consoled you?

DOUGLAS

You know what? It did. And I'm with Kate on this one. No one gives a shit about real writing.

KATE

I didn't say that.

DOUGLAS

Yeah but you wrote this phony thing and you're going to act like it's real and I think that's smart. I mean what the fuck are we doing, anyway? Fiction is a dying art form. And we're just eating our hearts out, while we throw ourselves off a cliff. But you could make a lot of money with this. And you know what, Martin? Hearing that Leonard is a plagiarist did, it consoled me. See you clowns next week.

He goes. Martin looks at Izzy and Kate.

KATE

It doesn't console me.

IZZY

You know what? I don't believe it. Leonard's no fraud.

MARTIN

Well, I think he did it.

IZZY

I don't.

MARTIN

I do.

KATE

And I think you're just looking for yet another excuse not to show him your writing.

MARTIN

What did you say?

KATE

You heard me.

MARTIN

If I'm not showing him my writing, it's because I don't care what he thinks about my writing. Particularly now.

KATE

Why because your message from the gods is so precious?

MARTIN

Every fucking corner of everything you write is precious if it isn't why would you write it? Don't answer that don't answer it because I know it's not a universally held truth but for some people constructing a UNIVERSE out of LANGUAGE is a timeless and reverential act, not an unholy excuse to fuck with people's heads. So, no. I don't care to show him my writing.

KATE

Writers aren't people.

MARTIN

What?

KATE

You said SOME PEOPLE for SOME PEOPLE writing is all this whatever but let me tell you something: WRITERS ARE NOT PEOPLE. That has NEVER been more clear.

She goes. Izzy and Martin sit in silence.

IZZY

Well. I'm going to take off.

MARTIN

I don't want you to take off.

IZZY

Yeah you do.

MARTIN

No! I don't. I don't. I don't.

IZZY

Martin.

She kisses him, then picks up a page of his story from where it drifted under the couch, two scenes ago. She hands it to him.

IZZY

You have things to do.

She goes. He looks at it.

Blackout.

Scene Eight

All are there. Leonard and Kate square off.

LEONARD

Is he coming?

KATE

He's actually not coming. No. He decided that he didn't have the money to do this right now. He was going to buy my half of the class, that was the deal, because I was...

LEONARD

Because you're quitting writing.

KATE

Yeah I decided not to do that.

LEONARD

So you're staying? Is that the earth-shattering announcement you are making to the group?

KATE
(a beat)
Yes that is the earth-shattering announcement I am making to the group.

LEONARD

There's some good stuff here. Fresh and muscular. And the speed is impressive. I'm glad to have seen this. It's shown me something. Why don't you tell him.

KATE

I will.
They look at each other

LEONARD

Good.

He turns to the others

LEONARD

Anybody got anything? Martin?

MARTIN

I do. Yes I do.

LEONARD

Really?

MARTIN

Yes I do. And before I hand it over I would like to politely ask at this juncture not to be called a pussy. I'm serious. It's unnecessary and the point has been thoroughly examined. I do have something to present to the group and to you, actually that's more the point isn't it; here, Leonard, is my soul carefully articulated and wrapped up in a neatly typed bow, for you to do with as you will, and I know you will behave responsibly toward this exceptionally precious gift that I am presenting you today. So the answer is yes. Yes, I have some pages. Here.

He hands about twenty pages. Leonard looks at him, looks at it. He weighs it in his hand, laughs a moment, looks at Martin.

LEONARD

Pussy.

Martin shakes his head, turns away. He can't watch Leonard read. Leonard reads the first page. The others watch. Leonard drops the page on the floor. He continues to read. He paces a little, as he reads, expressionless. Martin is in agony but he cannot look. Leonard drops another page. The others look at each other, not knowing what this means. Leonard drops another page. He continues to read, then stops himself. He rubs his eyes.

LEONARD
Unmistakable.

Martin turns to look at him, startled. All the others look at him too

MARTIN
What's that supposed to mean?

LEONARD
Who's seen this?

MARTIN
Nobody. You.

LEONARD
And you wrote it.

MARTIN
Yes of course I wrote it. I wrote it this week.

LEONARD
It's... very good.

MARTIN
Fuck you.

LEONARD
Fuck you too. How'd you get here anyway?

MARTIN
What?

LEONARD
Here, how did you get here? Am I not speaking English?

MARTIN
What do you mean "here?"

LEONARD
Here in my class, moron. Here. With me.

MARTIN
I knew Kate from before and she was already in the class and she said you were supposedly, the class was supposed to be so great to get in—

LEONARD
Yes yes I know this—

MARTIN
And she didn't know Douglas, we both had heard of him and I met Izzy at a party and she said she was in it too and that you were some kind of genius—

LEONARD
(impatient)
I'm not talking about them! I'm talking about you!

MARTIN
--so I knew that our high school English teacher knew you he always talked about how you guys were at Yale together so I wrote to him and asked him and he wrote to you and you let me in.

LEONARD
Your high school English teacher? What was his name?

MARTIN
Mr. Gladeau. Robert Gladeau.

LEONARD

(This does not ring any sort of bell)
Bob Gladeau? I let you in because you knew Bob Gladeau? That guy
was a moron. I let you in because he asked? I don't remember any of
this. Okay. Let's start over. Did I ever read anything you've written?

MARTIN

Yeah, you did. You read that.

LEONARD

I read this?

MARTIN

Well not exactly that part, the first twenty pages. Of that. It's the
beginning of the novel and that's further in.

LEONARD

Are the other pages as good as this?

MARTIN

Didn't you read them?

LEONARD

Fuck if I know.

MARTIN

You don't remember? You don't remember any of this?

LEONARD

Listen, Martin, I just spent two weeks in Somalia and since the day I
came back this one
(indicates Izzy)
--has been fucking my brains out so no, I don't remember much
right now! I don't think I read it. There is no way I would have
forgotten--listen this is good. You know this is good.

Martin looks at Izzy. Izzy won't look at him.

LEONARD

Is this all of it?

MARTIN
(distracted)
I'm sorry—

LEONARD

Stay with me, Martin. This is a novel, it's part of a novel, how much of it is written?

MARTIN
(detached)
Five hundred and sixteen pages.

LEONARD

What else do you have? And don't tell me nothing, I'll know you're lying. How much writing have you got stuffed in drawers and jamming up the circuits on your computer. How many pages do you have that you haven't shown a fucking soul.

MARTIN
(depressed)
A couple of thousand.

LEONARD

Well, you're a regular Emily Dickinson. Without the charm. Welcome to the land of the living, Emily. I want to see all of it. Now, right now. Go fire up the printer.

MARTIN

Why?

LEONARD

What do you care why. I just told you, you're a loser no more.

MARTIN

You don't know what you're talking about. You've been telling me and and and ALL OF US that we don't know shit--for weeks! You told Douglas to hang it up and go to Hollywood!

DOUGLAS

Don't drag me into this.

MARTIN

You are in it! We are all in it, we all paid five thousand dollars to be in it and he--doesn't know shit!

LEONARD

Are you sure you want to doubt my word right now?

MARTIN

I don't believe you've been fucking her all week. I don't believe it!

LEONARD

(laughing)

What?

MARTIN

She said she didn't. She told me—

IZZY

Martin--

LEONARD

Well, I don't know what she told you but I got no reason to make it up.

He goes back to reading Martin's story. Martin turns to Izzy.

MARTIN

I don't believe him. I don't.

IZZY

Can we take this somewhere else?

MARTIN

No! Answer the question!

IZZY

What's the question?

A beat.

MARTIN

Did you lie to me?

IZZY

Oh come on Martin. It wasn't much of a lie. Nobody believed it
except you.

Leonard looks up, around the room.

LEONARD

Are we done with the soap opera? Are we ready to get back to work?

MARTIN

No. No. I'm not doing this.

KATE

Martin.

MARTIN

He doesn't know anything! Why should I let him, why should any
of us-hasn't it occurred to any of you that he's so mean to us because
he's over! He can't do it anymore if he ever could and this is, it's
just-power, it's the only power he has anymore, to destroy, and the
thing he wants to destroy is young writers. It's TWISTED. And
we're so desperate, it's pathetic actually, we're so desperate that we're

just sitting here letting him-letting him destroy our hope and our curiosity and our talent and our dreams and why? It's NOTHING to him, he's, God, plus plus he's done so many drugs he can't even remember what he's read from one instant to the next plus he's UNETHICAL which I know it's a joke to even bring that up, that's how low ethics have fallen but I don't care he's UNETHICAL and a bad teacher and now I'm supposed to what, just jump up and down for joy because he's said 'oh, there's an unmistakable-'

LEONARD

Careful. That bit might be true.

MARTIN

Nothing you say is true. You're a plagiarist. You're just a fucking plagiarist.

> *Silence. Leonard laughs a little to himself, picks up the pages, flips through them.*

LEONARD

Yeah okay. You probably never told off your own father so you definitely needed to get that off your chest.

MARTIN

Fuck you.

LEONARD

And I'm glad to provide the opportunity for you. Feels good, doesn't it, spewing the truth, the truth is like a great fuck, it's one of the few remaining reasons to get out of bed in the morning. It's not for everybody, some people are so crippled they can't stand the truth, but for those of us who partake, nothing else really comes close. But you know what? All those other people, who can't stand the truth? They're going to be a problem for you. This is why: You're a fucking nobody. Who are your parents? Nobody. Who are your connections? NOBODY. Where'd you go to school? It isn't Harvard Princeton or Yale, so wherever you went? It DOESN'T MATTER. You're no Douglas, Martin. You're a talented nobody, everybody is going to hate you. I mean, you'll get this published, and it will get some attention but not what it should, and then you'll write a second novel, which will mess up your brain like nothing you've ever lived through, it will be the worst three years of your life, writing that second novel; you'll feel like you're in the ninth circle of hell, where the betrayers of Christ are frozen in eternal cannibalistic silence, only it's not flesh you'll be consuming, it's your mind. Maybe a few years after the second novel you'll be on to something with your third and you'll finally get into one of the big writer's colonies but your bitterness at having been rejected fifteen fucking times will take a lot of the fun out of that. You'll start to hate everyone out there who's more successful than you; what you feel for Douglas right now is nothing compared to what's coming. But the work will be good! Everyone will keep telling you how good the writing is! It's too good to be mistaken and that will become the bane of your existence. You might or might not get nominated for an occasional award. But you'll never make any money. Hollywood will start to look like something pretty good right about then but you won't feel like sucking up to them either so you'll waste months of your life wandering around that hellhole of a city wondering why so many hacks can make a go of it out there but you can't get arrested. You'll end up taking a university job so you can pay off your credit cards, which you ran up like some fucking woman all those years you let yourself get sucked into the writing, and then you'll be really screwed. One year of teaching and you'll get so sick of how stifling and boring and utterly pointless it all is, teaching writing to a bunch of hyper-privileged droning children, you'll start drinking even more than you already are, you'll start fucking your students, even the freshmen, especially the freshmen, they're the ones who haven't been ruined yet, and they'll be so in love with your genius their adoration will be like a drug and why not? Why the fuck not. The work is still great! You're a fucking artist! You have to feel something to write, something more than just bitterness and contempt for the idiots you write for, the biggest problem with being a writer finally is that ALL YOUR READERS ARE HUMAN BEINGS AND THE HUMAN RACE IS...

(a long silence)

You'll get fired for fucking undergrads, which is apparently against the law now. One of those undergraduates will make a reckless, devastating claim which too many people will want to believe by them. Things will continue to spiral. Your few remaining friends--maybe Douglas here, or Kate--will lend you a hand for old time's sake. You'll let them. And then you'll take on a few editing gigs, to make ends meet, and you'll be good at it and people will like it, they turned you into a servant, that will make them all feel great, and you'll get more and more editing work, and then you'll teach private writing seminars, which will feel like shit for a while until you realize that you really could do something, you could help the ones worth helping, if you only take on the best. The best students. And that will make it better. But you'll still be a fucking servant. Because at the moment in your life when someone said, you're a talented nobody but I'm going to help you? You said I don't need help.

(a beat.)

Class is over.

He goes.

Blackout.

Scene Nine

The walls open and we are in Leonard's apartment. A rat's nest of papers and books. A ritual African mask hangs on the wall. An exquisite bronze Buddha is wedged between books on one of the shelves. The place is cluttered with the detritus of a passionately undisciplined and curious mind. In the midst of it all, a desk with a typewriter, covered with papers, and an overstuffed couch.

The sound of a buzzer being pushed relentlessly.

After a moment, Leonard appears. He wears a bathrobe over sweatpants. He answers the door. Martin is there.

He is a mess.

MARTIN
I have to talk to you.

LEONARD
Yeah, well, kid, you know, now is not a good time.

MARTIN
Then we'll just, you know, have to make this fast.
            (a pause)
I I I--I—

LEONARD
This is fast?

MARTIN
Look, it's not easy for me to be here.

LEONARD
It's not easy for me, either. I'm busy!

He glances over his shoulder, toward the bedroom.

MARTIN
I'm sure. No, I'm sure you are. But I, I I I—

LEONARD
MARTIN, I don't want to be indiscreet but I'm busy here. You understand? I'm busy.

MARTIN
You have someone here with you.

LEONARD
What gave you that idea.

MARTIN
No, it's fine, I, it's fine.

LEONARD
Thanks. So if you don't mind—

MARTIN
I need my money. We were supposed to get ten weeks, and you only gave us four and I paid five thousand. If you aren't going to finish the class, that's three thousand dollars. I need it back.

LEONARD
Seriously. Do we have to do this now?

MARTIN
I have to have that money.

A beat. Leonard sighs.

LEONARD
Well—

Kate appears in the doorway behind him, wearing one of his shirts.

KATE

It's okay, Leonard, I have to take off anyway.

LEONARD

No, no no no—

KATE

Leonard. We've been at it for two days. I'm sore!

KATE

Hi, Martin.

MARTIN

Kate.

KATE

Yes, hello.

She goes to the couch and picks up her bra.

KATE

Where did I leave my panties, do you remember?

LEONARD

The kitchen?

KATE

That's right.

She goes. Leonard looks at Martin.

LEONARD

You missed the boat, Martin. She's an animal. This is the thing, the thing about feminists: You catch one, when she's right about to pop, it's like, I couldn't get her to stop and I'm not kidding, she's sucking my balls so hard I'm seeing stars giving birth to planets on the astral plane—

MARTIN

STOP STOP. STOP.

LEONARD

Oh, are you squeamish about sex? Because she sure isn't.

Kate reappears, holds up her panties.

KATE

I'll be right back.

She goes into the bedroom. Leonard looks at the door, looks at Martin, looks at the door.

LEONARD

You know what, Martin? I'm sorry about your situation, whatever it is, but this is a bad time.

He starts to follow Kate

MARTIN

I'm not leaving without that money. I don't care about whatever new depravity you have managed to inflict on someone I care about. It doesn't matter. I have no place to live and I have no money and I will become a homeless person in this god awful city if I don't get that money and I'm not leaving here without it.

He sits on the couch.

LEONARD

Why were you even in my class?

What?

LEONARD

Why did you even sign up? You walked out even before you walked in.

MARTIN

I didn't walk out, you walked out—

LEONARD

You walked out.

Kate opens the doorway and comes out, putting clothes on.
Both turn and look at her.

KATE

Leonard, I need a favor.

She gives him a long wet kiss.

KATE

I have to talk to Martin for a minute.

LEONARD

You want me to go take a shower?

KATE

Could you?

LEONARD

I could use one after that.

KATE

Thanks.

Leonard looks back at Martin, shakes his head and goes.

MARTIN

What, what are you doing here?

KATE

You know what? That is a stupid question.

MARTIN

You slept with him?

KATE

Wow. We went so far beyond that, it's not really worth answering that one either.

MARTIN

You hate him!

KATE

I wouldn't say that, no.

MARTIN

You think he's disgusting! He IS disgusting! And now you're here-
-doing--things--with that, that, FUCK ME I cannot think of words BAD ENOUGH to describe that TOXIC PIECE OF SHIT ASSHOLE. It was bad enough that Izzy was sleeping with him. That was bad enough.

KATE

But it's worse if I do? Why?

MARTIN

Because you--have a brain!

KATE

There are other parts of my body as well, Martin, a fact you never quite noticed. But guess who did.

MARTIN

Is that why you're doing this? To get back at me?

KATE

Wow. That is classic.

MARTIN

Well, is it? Is that why you kicked me out?

KATE

I kicked you out because I finally grew a spine! I kicked you out because you were completely using me! I was the one, I TOLD you about the whole seminar because I knew you would let yourself just disappear, if someone didn't-- and then you you you had no respect. I took care of you. I was taking care of you and you took advantage—

MARTIN
(overlap)

I know. I know. I know! Because you care about me.

KATE

Well --I did

MARTIN

You still do.

KATE

Oh no I don't.

MARTIN

I may not deserve it.

KATE

You don't.

MARTIN

But it's there nonetheless. You can't tell me it isn't. Come on, Kate.

I'm an idiot but the truth remains that you--you-you're—

KATE

Oh. Oh no. Oh no no no no—

MARTIN

You're--night and day.

KATE

Okay, Martin.

MARTIN

You're stars and moon and wind.

He kisses her.

KATE

I said okay!

Beat.

MARTIN

Kate, come on. We were good together. And I admit, I blew it.
My head was so, that class was so poisonous, Leonared was so
poisonous—

KATE

Don't start on Leonard, a lot of what he said worked. He actually got
me to write something new and fresh—

MARTIN

And fraudulent—

KATE

Fraud is a way of life, in a capitalist culture. Especially in the arts.
You should hear what Leonard has to say about it.

MARTIN

I don't want to talk about Leonard!

KATE

Then why do you keep bringing him up?

MARTIN

Why do I, why do you, you you you—

KATE

He's done a lot for all of us. He got Douglas a meeting with the Weinsteins. He introduced Izzy to Salman Rushdie who is a huge flirt and wants to help her with her drug whore book. And he set me up with this guy in prison who has one hell of a story. Random House needs someone to ghost write it for him.

MARTIN

So Leonard got you a job as a ghost writer! And you took it.

KATE

Martin, I would be crazy not to take that job and I thought it was pretty nice of Leonard to set it up. He was, actually, an asshole about it. He managed to mention to my editor about six times that I had written a really shitty story about a girl who was obsessed with Jane Austen. But he was nice enough about the Cubano cross dresser. And I like this job. I think it's a good start for someone like me. I'm excited about it.

MARTIN

A ghost writer.

KATE

I knew you'd look down on it. You know what? You have a screw loose, Martin, you really do. He stood there and told all of us how good you are. He said it. And you may think he's a fucking asshole, but you know in your heart he would never lie about something like that. And you're still, you're just still eating your soul out over what?

Why don't you just live it, Martin?

MARTIN

So what are you, you you actually LIKE him?

KATE
(a breath)
Life is complicated. People are complicated. If you can't figure that
out, you'll never be much of a writer, I don't care what Leonard says.
Honestly he's convinced you're the next big thing. I think it's some
sort of narcissistic projection. Boys boys boys you just never get
enough of yourselves, do you?

> *She goes to the door, and leaves. He sits there, alone. He
> thinks about going after her. He doesn't. He looks around
> the room. He goes to the wall and looks at the artifacts
> crammed in among the books. He goes to look at the
> Buddha, on the desk. While there, he starts to poke about.
> He looks at Leonard's pencils. He looks at pages that have
> been left on the desk. He looks up, to see if anyone is
> looking. He starts to read.*

> *Like Leonard, he drops a page to the floor, still reading.*

> *Leonard appears in the doorway. He watches for a
> moment as Martin reads.*

LEONARD

Okay, that's enough.

> *He grabs the pages from Martin, who backs up, startled.*

LEONARD

Get out of here.

MARTIN

I was just looking at—

LEONARD

You were just *spying*, you little rat. You were just--give me that. GET YOUR HANDS OFF THAT.

Martin is still trying to get the pages together. He shoves him aside. They stare at each other.

LEONARD

Sorry. I don't like for people to look at that.

MARTIN

Why not?

LEONARD

That's hilarious, coming from you. You'd spend five thousand dollars on a writing seminar, and then not let anyone read your shit. Take your money and get out of here.

He finishes writing a check, holds it out. Martin doesn't take it.

MARTIN

Your novel's really good.

LEONARD

Wow. Thanks, SpongeBob. I'll alert the New York Times.

MARTIN

You're not a plagiarist.

LEONARD

Jesus. How long is this going to go on? Because if you're thinking we're actually going to have a conversation, I'm getting a drink.

He goes into the kitchen. Martin goes back to the desk, finds the pages, and starts to read again. He reads eagerly, fascinated. Leonard reenters, balks, then bolts into the room.

LEONARD

Did you think I was kidding? I do not want you reading that! No one is allowed to read that!

MARTIN

Why not?

LEONARD

I don't have to tell you why not! Give me the fucking pages, Martin.

Martin takes a step back, holding them.

MARTIN

Why don't you show this to anybody? Why do you let people think you're not writing?

LEONARD

I don't give a shit what people think.

MARTIN

Yes you do, you put on this whole--act--that you're an embittered old psychopath—

LEONARD

Hey. That's no act.

MARTIN

Who can't write! You gave us that whole speech, boo hoo, my career is over and I'm stuck with these losers who can't write--and meanwhile you, you're, you can, this is great. This is, like-- It's like a nineteenth century novel. It's....

He stops. He has no words.

LEONARD

This the twenty-first century. And I actually don't like people scraping their eyeballs on my words.

MARTIN

Why not?

He takes the pages from Martin, and goes to the desk. Picks up all the pages and dumps them in a drawer.

LEONARD
(beat, simple)

I have no skin anymore. Once it's written I can't--live with it. I can't sit in offices and talk to people about it. I can't look at "cover art." I can't talk to editors; these people are so nice and I just want to strangle them, it's completely unfair. It makes more sense to just put it out on the sidewalk and let it blow away. Not blow away, not--Jesus. I have no skin. After I write, I want to evaporate. And you don't evaporate, you're still here, your body is just, it takes up so much space. Plus, there's so much noise. Novels need silence. Trust me. It's not the writing that's the problem. It's everything else.
(then)
That kid was a liar. To be called a thief of words. I can't even. That was thirty two years ago and I can't even...
(beat)
Here's your check.

MARTIN

That's bullshit. What you just, that is the stupidest shit I've ever heard come out of your mouth. And as you know many really fucked up stupid things have come out of your mouth.

LEONARD
(overlap)

Yeah yeah yeah. Nevertheless, everything I tell you is true.

MARTIN

Get away from that desk.

LEONARD

This is my apartment, you moron.

MARTIN

I don't care. Get away from that desk or I will hit you on the head with the Buddha.

He picks up the Buddha and tries to figure out how to do that. Leonard considers this, then stands.

LEONARD

I need a drink anyway.

He stands and goes to the other side of the room, pours himself a drink. Martin goes to the desk drawer and takes out the novel. He sets it on the desk. He looks at it.

MARTIN

This doesn't belong to you.

LEONARD

Really.

MARTIN

It is not you, and it's not even of you. It is not yours.

LEONARD

Then whose is it?

MARTIN

It is itself. And you are not hiding it in a desk and just burying it alive. It's immoral.

LEONARD
Please. Don't talk to me about morality.

MARTIN
I'm taking this away from you, so you can't hurt it anymore.

He picks up the novel and edges toward the door.

LEONARD
Why'd you come over here anyway?

MARTIN
I came over to--get my money.

LEONARD
Then why are you leaving without it. I offered it to you twice, you never even looked at it, you just told me endlessly yet again that I'm full of shit. I mean, I am well aware I'm full of shit, why do you need to go over and over it? What more do you want from me? You want my balls?

MARTIN
No I don't want your balls. God, I don't even know what you're talking about half the time!

Leonard reaches onto the desk and finds a folded sheaf of papers. He holds it up.

LEONARD
Here.

MARTIN
What's that?

LEONARD
I finally read those pages that idiot Bob Gladeau sent me. The first twenty pages of your masterpiece. I did a line edit for you, show you

what you got.

He holds out the pages, then indicates that Martin had better give him his own pages back. They exchange pages. Leonard goes to the desk and puts his novel in a drawer. Martin sits, and reads.

MARTIN
(after a beat)
So you think I...

LEONARD
You're just hearing too many words.

Martin continues to read. Leonard goes to the bottle of booze, fills up his own and a second glass. Martin continues to read. After a moment he looks up.

MARTIN
This is--fantastic.

LEONARD
It really is the only way to learn anything about writing, to have a decent editor go through it word by word for you. Help you see what it is, what you meant. What you didn't even know you meant.

MARTIN
No, it does it really....

LEONARD
Yeah, you hear it different, you hear the ding.

MARTIN
Thank you.

LEONARD
Don't mention it.

(a beat)
So. You want to try this?

Martin looks at him, nervous, looks around.

MARTIN
What, try what?

LEONARD
Relax Romeo you're not my type. I'm just saying. I'll work with you.

MARTIN
Really? Well. What, um, what--what, what would that mean?

LEONARD
I'm not exactly an unknown quantity, Martin What do you think it would mean?

MARTIN
I have no idea.

LEONARD
It would mean, I will fuck you up in so many different ways you won't even know who you are anymore. That seminar was the prelude. You want to make me your servant, you got Mephistopheles in your pocket. That's what it means. So what is it? How serious are you? You want to be a writer, or not?

Martin looks at him.   Leonard holds out his drink.   After a long moment Martin reaches out to take it.

Blackout.